Introduction

The origins of the hobby of keeping fish in containers goes back for very many centuries. It is generally considered that it was first started by the Chinese who kept fish in earthenware pots. In those early days the fish did not survive too long because little was known about water chemistry or the importance of such matters as aeration and filtration. It was in fact to be many centuries before these aspects were fully appreciated. As a result millions of fish died simply because of the owners' ignorance of these needs. Even today, with all the modern technology available to fishkeepers, this same fact is true especially with coldwater species, such as goldfish, which have suffered more than any other group. All too often well-wishing parents will purchase a goldfish for their children and place it in a small globe container, complete with a little gravel and maybe a ceramic arch or the like. Frequently, within days the poor fish is found floating on the surface or lying on the gravel substrate, its inner being having departed to wherever all goldfish go in the hereafter!

Sadly, this scenario may be repeated a number of times before the owners either abandon fishkeeping or decide to learn a little more about why their pets keep dying. The same is true of a number of tropical fish keepers. They may well purchase more equipment than the goldfish owner, but unless they understand what this equipment must do, they can still run into all

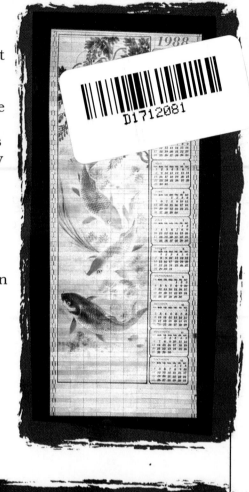

The calendar above and the stamp below show the Chinese love of fancy fishes. Probably the Chinese started aquarium fishkeeping 3,000 years ago!

← The Chinese developed the first fancy strains of goldfish. These strains are still available now.

↓ Many fishes only do well in schools, like these Cardinal Tetras, *Paracheirodon axelrodi.*

This luxurious ivory statue shows an oriental fisherman carrying colorful Japanese carp (koi or nishikigoi). ←

sorts of problems. For example, simply siting the aquarium in the wrong place can result in a chain of disasters which may wipe out the entire tank population, irrespective of what technology has been incorporated into it. The equipment may not be able to cope with the changing conditions created by the siting of the tank unit.

Likewise, the number of fish that can be placed into an aquarium is not a matter of chance, but is critical once a given stock rate is reached. Some fish will survive in water of a given temperature, where others will be uncomfortable at the least, and may die at worst. Apart from any other factor, the temperature will have a considerable effect on the colors displayed by fish.

Yet another very important aspect in keeping fish is whether or not they are compatible. If the wrong species are placed together the result will be that some may eat the others. Even if this does not happen some fish may become so stressed by worry created by their tank mates that they become ill and die anyway.

All in all there are very many things that can and do go wrong in an aquarium, so even the experts can have problems. However, just taking a little time to understand that when you set up an aquarium you are creating an entire world in miniature will go a long way to ensuring your problems are minimal. This will then mean you can relax and enjoy the tremendous benefits that go with owning a nicely stocked and furnished aquarium.

Apart from the obvious enjoyment gained from simply admiring the fish, you will find much pleasure in planning the aquascene and improving this as time goes by. It is also a fact that if you sit and watch your fish this will help relieve the day to day stress created in our modern world. The therapeutic value of fish in particular is well documented. Fish are not at all difficult to look after if the aquarium has been correctly set up. Maintaining the conditions they need to keep them fit and healthy will not take up a lot of time.

While the principles that govern the maintenance of an aquarium apply broadly to all fishes, there are certain differences that must be understood between various groups of fish. For example, you cannot put marine species in a freshwater aquarium, because each type of fish has evolved to live in a specific type of water. Likewise, coldwater fish will not fare very well under tropical conditions, nor vice versa. There are, of course, no sudden changes from one type of water to another, which means that there are in fact some fish that can survive in either salt or fresh water within given tolerances.

There are also fish that are able to live in both cold and warm waters, but these do not

◆ Siamese Fighting Fish, *Betta splendens*, are gorgeous but only one male can be kept in an aquarium or they will fight.

◀ An aquarium must be a thing of beauty and appealing to its owner. Since *beauty lies in the eyes of the beholder*, different kinds of aquariums appeal to different types. Visit your aquarium shop and see what appeals to you.

Guppies are available in many colors and fin shapes. They are peaceful, easy to breed and fairly hardy. An ideal fish for the beginner. ➡

comprise the mainstream of fish kept by the aquarist, though examples of them, such as goldfish, guppies and mollies, are extremely popular. This is because they are so adaptable and thus regarded as being very hardy species. However, this book is written for those who wish to keep freshwater tropical fish. To fully understand what this term implies it is worthwhile considering each of the various habitats that make up the main fishkeeping groups.

☛ Marine fishes do NOT live long in fresh water. The techniques of maintaining a freshwater aquarium differ greatly from saltwater tank management. Saltwater tanks are not for beginning aquarists. This is *Holocanthus ciliaris*.

▶ Piranhas have no place in the beginners' aquarium. They are dangerous...more dangerous in an aquarium than in nature.

A well maintained aquarium like this one belonging to Stefan Kornobi features Cardinal Tetras and Rummy-nosed Tetras, with lovely deep green plants. An aquarium must be beautiful, sweet-smelling and interesting. ☛

Fish Habitats

MARINE OR SALTWATER: Examples of this habitat are of course the seas and oceans of the world. However, there are some lakes that can be of a saltwater base. Generally, conditions in the marine environment are very stable because of the large mass and depths of the waters involved. Fish that live in salt water have adapted to cope with the high salinity of their watery world. The concentration of salt in the water means their body is constantly losing water as a result of a process known as osmosis. This means they have to drink copious amounts of water to compensate, otherwise

they would soon be drained of liquid.

Because of the need to maintain very stable conditions, and because of the need to prepare salt water, keeping marine fish is more complex than keeping freshwater fish. Further, because few marine species have been bred in captivity, they cost considerably more than their freshwater relatives. Most are taken from wild habitats, so there are further complications in acclimatizing them to the aquarium.

FRESHWATER HABITATS: These comprise the rivers, streams and lakes of the world. They can vary considerably in their make-up, but in broad terms they are either acidic or alkaline, depending whether or not they

● *Chaetodon austriacus* is a marine fish. Because it, and most other marine fish, are not being bred in captivity, their cost is significantly higher than that of freshwater fish.

◀ The Hornet Cichlid, *Pseudotropheus crabro*, from Lake Malawi, requires hard water containing special salts, but NOT sea salts. Many fishes have special requirements. If you are interested in Malawi cichlids, get a good book on the subject.

Another cichlid from Lake Malawi, this specimen is characterized by a rarely seen lyretail. The pointed fins indicate this is a male. Cichlids from Lake Malawi are very territorial and should NOT be kept by beginners. ◀

are flowing over a substrate that is of organic or calcareous content. The salt content of freshwater species is greater than that of the water in which they live, which means they are continually absorbing water through osmosis. The result is that they drink little and get rid of excess water via a copious, dilute urine. This is thus the complete reverse of the situation found in saltwater species. In both marine and

◆ A pair of Black Mollies, *Poecilia latipinna*. The female (the upper fish) has a fan-shaped anal fin while the male has a pointed anal fin which is used to assist in fertilization.

◗ The Zebra Danio, *Brachydanio rerio*, is a recommended fish for beginners. They are hardy, peaceful and eat most aquarium foods.

The King of the Aquarium is the Discusfish, *Symphysodon* sp. This specimen is a beautiful turquoise blue hybrid developed by Gan Aquarium Fish Farm in Singapore. ◆

freshwater habitats the temperatures can vary, so there are the ice cold salt waters of the arctic oceans, and the beautifully warm tropical oceans. Likewise, there are the tropical rivers of the equatorial regions, and the much colder rivers of temperate areas of our planet. In the latter regions the water temperature can range from moderately warm in the summer to very cold in the winter, whereas in the tropics the temperature fluctuation between winter and summer is far less extreme.

This is why species such as guppies and goldfish are able to survive in both heated and unheated aquariums, though basically a goldfish is a coldwater fish and the guppy a tropical. By appreciating these basic differences in both the physiology of fish and the many varied types of habitat, you are less likely to place the wrong fish in the watery world you create within your aquarium unit. Put another way, the aquarist creates the conditions needed for the type of fish he or she wishes to maintain.

In this book you will find all of the basic information you will need in order to establish an aquarium containing a workable community of tropical freshwater species. The conditions that will be created will accommodate many types of fish, both livebearing and egglaying species that are suited to being kept by beginners. These fish represent a very popular group of species in aquatic circles. Most are very reasonably priced, so are ideally suited to the first time fishkeeper.

Many are also water condition tolerant, by which is meant that they are quite hardy and will not keel over and die if they are subjected to conditions that are less than ideal. This said, you should always try to maintain superb water conditions, because only in this way will you get maximum pleasure from your hobby. It is the most cost efficient way to proceed. You will not be having to replace dead fish, and you will be able to breed many of the species you keep. Most freshwater tropical fish are in fact obtained from stock bred in commercial fish farms. They are thus quite familiar with the aquarium and not stressed by it. By keeping commercially bred freshwater tropicals you are not taking from the wild, so if you are a keen conservationist these are the fish to own.

▲ A blotched Angelfish, *Pterophyllum* sp. This is a tank-raised hybrid which keeps losing black coloration until it is pure golden. These are not very easy fish to keep in the beginner's aquarium.

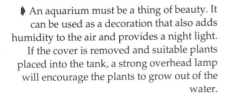

◆ The Red Oscar, *Astronotus ocellatus*, is a red sport developed in the aquarium. The original fish come from Brazil.

◗ An aquarium must be a thing of beauty. It can be used as a decoration that also adds humidity to the air and provides a night light. If the cover is removed and suitable plants placed into the tank, a strong overhead lamp will encourage the plants to grow out of the water.

The four tanks shown on this page merely suggest variations possible with a standard 20 gallon long aquarium. There are also 20 gallon tanks which are shorter but higher. Ask your dealer what he suggests for your pocketbook and space available.

Selecting an Aquarium

When considering what aquarium unit is best suited to your needs the first thing you should bear in mind is that it will represent the entire world to your pet fish. It should therefore be as large as you can possibly afford. From a practical viewpoint there are only benefits in having a large aquarium.

1. The water quality of a large unit will change only very slowly when compared to a small tank. The greater the volume the greater its buffering capacity to resist chemical changes in the water.

2. The temperature is far less susceptible to fluctuation. This means the heater(s) will not be working continually to raise the temperature to

the desired level. The greater the volume of water the longer it will retain heat.

3. The larger the tank the more fish it will be able to sustain.

4. The larger tank will give the fish more room to swim in and will allow you greater scope to furnish the unit with plants and rocks.

5. Such an aquarium will be easier to maintain simply because its water properties will remain more stable for a longer period.

6. From a viewing standpoint the large unit is esthetically pleasing. The very small aquarium is hardly noticed in the average room and provides little scope to be developed as a hobby.

Generally, most aquarists will own at least one good sized display tank as well as a number of smaller units which are used for breeding and for quarantining or hospitalizing ailing fish. A keen hobbyist may have twenty or more tanks. The beginner is advised to have one good display tank and maybe a couple of smaller units which are used for quarantine purposes and for growing young plants until they are strong enough to be placed in the display tank.

Tank Capacities

Trying to define how large is a large aquarium is akin to asking how long is a piece of string. Nonetheless we can place some dimensions to this matter. As a rule of thumb you can work on the basis that a tank with a water capacity of about 18 US gal (15 UK) would

be a nice size for a beginner. Any smaller than this and it will not have the appearance or hobby flexibility to be developed to the extent you might wish. If you can afford a larger tank then by all means get one, but do not purchase a smaller one even though you may find that experienced aquarists often use such tanks. In these instances they are probably using them as species tank, meaning devoted to a single species, or they are breeding tanks. Further, such people are very experienced at maintaining

The four aquatic scenes shown on this page may suggest formats for your own aquarium. Each tank must have a hood, lights, heater, filter and stand. Your local aquarium dealer is the best person to suggest what is best for your particular needs.

◆ A Red-tailed Tuxedo Platy Variatus, a highly recommended fish for the beginner. This is a female as you can verify by the fan shaped anal fin.

This is a good view of a beginner's tank. Not too many fishes or plants, but the barbs and tetras will eventually chew off the thread-like fins of the gouramis and angelfish. ◆

excellent water conditions. It would be better to wait and start with a good sized unit than to rush into the hobby with a small aquarium that may well result in the sort of problems that might spoil all the fun you should experience.

To calculate the volume of an aquarium based on its dimensions is very simple. The length times the width times the depth equals the volume. Let us look at an example.

60 x 45 x 38cm = 102,600cm^3 (24 x 18 x 15in = 6,480in^3)

There are 3,785 cu cm in a US gal, so our example will hold:

102,600 divided by 3,785 = about 27 US gals

If you prefer to work in inches there are 231 in^3 to the US gal:

6,480 divided by 231 = about 28 gals

These are approximates, which is why an extra gallon appears on the latter volume.

If you want large fishes, you need a large tank. This tank is 100 gallons and contains a large albino Oscar, *Astronotus*, and an Arowana, *Osteoglossum bicirrhosum*.

◂ Discuss with a knowledgeable dealer the costs of the largest tank possible. Remember your tank needs a cover (hood), heater, filter, plants and fishes, as well as a stand upon which to place it.

This goldfish bowl is NOT satisfactory for more than one small goldfish or a large male Siamese Fighting Fish. ▸

Your selection of an aquarium stand depends upon the furniture in your home and the cost. The ideal is a closed cabinet in which paraphernalia can be stored out of sight. ◂

A small flat goldfish bowl is preferred to a long, tall one because it gets more oxygen.

Make sure that the aquarium fits perfectly on the aquarium stand. This should be done BEFORE you buy the tank and stand.

One manufacturer makes a plexiglas tank with a fitted canopy and stand which is beautiful but very expensive. ▸

An ideal small aquarium...but even this 10 gallon tank can weigh 100 pounds!

To convert between US, Imperial (British), and European capacities the following will be useful:
1 US gallon = 0.833 Imperial gal = 3.78 liters. 1 Imp gallon = 1.2 US gal = 4.55 liters; 1 Liter = 0.264 US gal = 0.22 Imp gal

It is crucial that you know the capacity of your aquarium because when adding medicines the dosage will be related to this. Excess medication could be fatal to the fish. It is also important that you know how much the unit weighs when it is full of water. You can calculate this by using the following guide:
1 US gal weighs 8.345 lbs or 3.8 kg; 1 Imp gal weighs 10 lb or 4.55 kg; 1 Liter weighs 1 kg or 2.2 lb

The weight of the filled unit will obviously be rather important if it is to be placed on a shelf or stand. Aquariums are deceptively heavy units. The supports should be tested carefully in advance, rather than taking the risk that the extra few pints might send everything crashing to the floor—or maybe even through the floorboards with a 25 gallon tank. The latter would be heavier than the average overweight man!

Of course the unit will also have rocks and gravel in it, but these will displace a quantity of the water, and the unit is never filled to the brim. Using the tank's potential capacity should be a good guide to its ultimate furnished weight.

Aquarium Shape

You will see in your pet or aquatic store all manner of aquarium shapes, but the best advice you can take is to purchase a good old fashioned rectangle. This offers you excellent visibility of the tank interior, it is easy to calculate capacities, and it presents no special problems. The tall round aquariums distort the view of the fish, and can create lighting and aeration problems. Bow fronted tanks are fashionable, but again they come with related problems of viewing. Further, with rounded units in the event the canopy breaks you may find it more difficult to obtain a suitable replacement. Housing the lights may also present problems with non-rectangular shapes, unless the unit comes complete with these.

Tanks are made of glass or plexiglas of varying qualities. The former are the most serviceable in terms of their life and properties. They do not scratch readily, so are easily cleaned. The better quality plexi-glas units are almost as good, but the low cost aquariums tend to yellow with age.

◆ Tropical fish can be real pets! This Oscar, *Astronotus ocellatus*, seems to be talking back to its owner.

◗ Every aquarium should have a top light and a covering of sorts for the top. Either the light can be fitted with the top or the top can merely be covered with a piece of glass.

➤ A more elaborate setup for the larger aquarium would be for the lights to be built into a hood. The hood would be hinged to make getting into the aquarium a simpler task.

With modern silicone bondings the handy person can of course make their own tank to maybe fit a special alcove. However, the average hobbyist is better advised to purchase a commercially made unit because it will be built to take the considerable pressure exerted by water on the tank panels.

I would not recommend obtaining a second hand unit made in the days when

◆ Every aquarium must have a hood or canopy on top. This keeps the tank clean, houses the light, prevents evaporation and prevents the fish from jumping out. Photo courtesy of Hagen.

◆ The hood or canopy should fit the tank perfectly and should be purchased at the same time you buy your tank.

◆ Do NOT use bottom gravel straight from the bag; wash it thoroughly first and put it in slowly.

◆ If you cannot afford a hood, get a hinged glass top upon which you can add a light.

◆ Once the gravel is in place, pat it to shape it so it slopes from back to front.

angle iron frames were common. These invariably leak because they have rusted, are usually scratched, and the iron may cause contamination to the water quality. Modern units may have polished metal casings, but these are usually for decoration rather than strength. They are invariably of a stainless steel or aluminum metals that are much less corrosive than iron.

You can purchase tanks with or without a canopy (hood) which houses the lighting, but the best packages usually come complete. This saves you a lot of messing around finding suitable fitments. The aquarium should also have a glass or plastic cover that fits over the water, under the canopy. This helps to conserve the heat, as well as preventing debris from falling into the water, or the fish jumping out. It will also reduce the quantity of water that is lost by surface evaporation. However, it must be kept very clean, otherwise it will greatly diminish the benefits gained from the aquarium lights.

A Red-tailed Platy Variatus male.

The Importance of the Water Surface

The most common reason why goldfish in a globe die rather rapidly is because they have insufficient oxygen, especially if two or three fish are placed into these antiquated containers. If you think of the globe, you will appreciate that it has a narrow neck, thus a reduced water surface. It is at the water/air interface that oxygen dissolves. The smaller the water surface, the less air it can absorb (and the less unwanted gases can dissipate), thus the less fish the container can support. As a general point, you can regard this as so irrespective of the volume of water under consideration.

Salt-and-Pepper Red Variatus Platy male.

A tall tank with a small surface cannot sustain anything like the same number of fish as a tank of the same volume, but which has a large surface area. Aquarists therefore calculate the number of fish a tank can support based on the surface. The generally accepted calculation for tropical fish is that you can have 2.5cm (1in) of fish (not including the tail) for every 75cm^2 (12in^2) of water surface.

Golden Wagtail Platy male.

If the tank is 60 x 38cm this gives a surface area of 2,280cm^2. Divided by 75, this will mean that the aquarium can house a total of 75cm (30in) of fish. This length can be divided by the average length of the species kept. However, when working out the stocking

Red Tuxedo Platy male.

Gold Velvet Tuxedo Swordtail male.

Peppermint Swordtail male.

Velvet Red Tuxedo Swordtail male.

Red Tuxedo Swordtail male.

Blood Red Albino Swordtail male.

level do bear in mind that you should make due allowance for growth. If you do not, you could find you are greatly exceeding the recommended levels, and problems could ensue. It is also worthy of mentioning that the stocking rate of a coldwater aquarium is half that of its tropical counterpart, so never stock a goldfish tank at the same rate as you would for tropical species.

You will no doubt notice that aquatic shops often stock at a much higher level than the figures quoted here. This is because if mechanical aeration and filtration is a feature of the tank, this will allow substantially more fish to be kept than in the unaerated tank. These aspects are considered in the following chapter together with cautionary comments on them.

For a fish to grow to its maximum potential and exhibit its colors to the full, it is of some importance that you do not overstock your aquarium. This is a fault of many aquarists. Size in fish is directly related to available swimming space and the level of population density in the water. The greater the population, the slower the growing rate—and the fish will not attain their potential size.

Where to Place the Aquarium

The location you choose for your aquarium should be selected with great care. A number of factors make this important.

1. Natural Light: You might think that natural sunlight would be beneficial for an aquarium, but this is not actually the case. In a natural

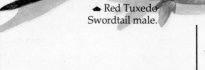

◀ A spawning trap for live-bearers should contain a very bushy plant so the babies can find a place to hide from their cannibalistic mother.

◆ Hagen Algae Magnets allow you to clean your aquarium glass without getting your hands wet.

You can clean the glass by hand with an algae cleaner wand, but the algae magnet is easier. ▶

The Hagen Aquarium Gravel Cleaner allows you to siphon the dirt from the aquarium floor. ▶

The Hagen Multi-Vac is battery powered so you don't need a siphon to clean the gravel. ▶

◀ When first setting up a tank the water must be conditioned by removing chloramine and chlorine, and starting microscopic life. Hagen makes FIN CARE for just this purpose.

◀ Hagen makes a siphon starter that saves the unpleasant sucking experience with which most siphons are started.

◀ There are combination planting sticks and cleaning wands available from Hagen.

habitat sunlight penetrates the water from above. The volume of the water is so large that the heat from the sun does not result in a sudden temperature change, but rather in one that is very slow and steady.

In the confines of an aquarium the sun's rays can rapidly increase the water temperature to an unacceptably high level. The overnight drop can then result in fluctuations that are far too rapid for the good health of your fish. Further, as the light will enter the tank from the front or rear panels,

◆ Once the rocks have been in the tank for a while, they usually develop an attractive coating of algae. This algae is helpful in keeping the water clean as well as providing an interesting snack for vegetarian fishes.

▶ When selecting your aquarium keep in mind that the sun's rays can be dangerous to an aquarium. If the back is to face a window, select a suitable opaque aquarium background.

The Sunshine Dragon, ◆
Hypostomus species

The Starry Night
Hypostomus. ➤

this will result in the plants growing toward the source of light rather than upwards, which would be natural in the wild and most desirable in the aquarium. This process, known as phototropism, is also applicable to the fish in some instances. They may swim on a slight angle.

Excess algal growth: Whilst the growth

of green algae is a desirable feature of an aquarium, you do not want this to be rampant. Bright sunlight directed on the aquarium will result not only in the viewing and side panels becoming covered with algae, but also the rocks. The water itself may be saturated with these microscopic organisms, and the effect will be a rapid build up in pollution as the algae die. This excess of algae is often seen in poorly sited and tended aquariums.

To avoid the problems inherent with natural sunlight, the tank should be located where it receives some natural light, but not an excessive amount. This means that near windows is a very bad location.

2. DRAFTS: The aquarium should not be placed where it will be exposed to cold drafts because these will obviously result in a cooling of the water. This will mean the heaters will continually be coming on and then switching off. Again, the resulting rapid fluctuations will not be healthy for the fish. Do not place the tank opposite or close to any doors or windows that might bring about this situation.

3. HEATER UNITS: For the same reasons of temperature fluctuation it is not wise to place an aquarium over or near a room heater of any kind.

4. VIEWING: You should ponder where you will generally be seated in relation to your tank so that you can gain the greatest viewing pleasure from it. Other aspects, such as the location of power outlets that will be

◆ Karl Schnell, the first man to breed (but not raise) *Pterophyllum altum*, the Giant Angelfish. He keeps his aquarium low so he can see it when he is seated. The blue jar contains the developing eggs of the Angelfish.

➥ The ideal Discus setup in some very expensive furniture! Cleanliness is a must in an aquarium like this.

needed, may also influence your final choice. Do not place the unit under a bookshelf or any other shelf that contains articles you may use on a regular basis. Sooner or later something will be dropped on the aquarium hood. Apart from shocking the fish you may well damage equipment.

Finally, bear in mind that you must have good access to the aquarium in order to attend to routine maintenance and partial water changes. If the access is poor this will tend to discourage doing chores, to the detriment of the whole ecosystem you are carefully trying to create.

◆ This magnificent aquarium is made in Italy by Aquarium Bologna. It comes complete with stand, pump, heater and filter. Your local pet shop may be able to get something like this for you.

◆ The newest kind of hybrid discus is Gan's Vertically Striped Discus. Gan may well be the most successful of all discus breeders in Singapore.

◀ An aquarium is an ideal hobby for young people...and it does NOT have to be very fancy to be enjoyed. The table upon which this aquarium is placed looks a bit skimpy. The 20-gallon aquarium weighs close to 200 pounds!

Aeration & Filtration

In order to best convey the importance of aeration and filtration in an aquarium just consider the following situation. Imagine outside of your home you had an enormous water container. In this water you attended to your bathing and washing. You also washed your clothes in it, and your pots and pans. Further, whenever you used the toilet this too was circulated into that same container. Finally, it was also the source of your drinking water! How long do you think you would use that container and remain healthy?

Now if the thought of that chills you, just

➡ Teach your children to keep their hands out of the aquarium when electrical gadgets are being installed.

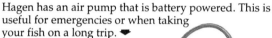

Hagen has an air pump that is battery powered. This is useful for emergencies or when taking your fish on a long trip. ➡

➡ Special air pumps running via vibrating membranes are available in at least 4 different sizes. Photo by Hagen.

➡ Air pumps running small inside filters must be matched. You don't want excessive air to interfere with the operation of the filter.

It's not how large the aquarium is that is important, but how DEEP it is, as depth creates back pressure and a more powerful pump is needed for deep tanks.

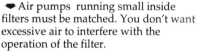

➡ Never remove a submergible electrical pump (or heater) unless it is disconnected.

imagine having to live in it as well! But this is exactly what many owners condemn their fish to do—again, especially the poor old goldfish living in a little goldfish globe. An aquarium is merely a closed water container, and unless it is serviced by aeration and filtration equipment the water will rapidly become polluted to the degree no fish could survive in it. You can of course

◀ A beautifully planted small aquarium for angelfish.

◀ Special aquariums built and outfitted for special fishes...like this aquarium specifically designed for housing (and breeding, hopefully) the Giant Angelfish, *Pterophyllum altum.*

Two of the world's great authorities on aquariums, the bearded Bernd Degen to the left and Murray Wiener. Degen is the Discus King of Europe; Wiener has a very successful aquarium shop in New Jersey. They both have the ability to recognize healthy fish at a glance...even before the sick fishes develop symptoms. ◀

overcome this situation by regular water changes, but these are time consuming and do not provide the stable environment needed to maintain fish at a peak of good health. This said, even with mechanical equipment it is prudent to do periodic partial water changes. However, these will largely be done as a safety measure, rather than from necessity as in a tank fitted with no equipment.

Aeration

As the name implies the main object of aeration is to increase the oxygen content of the water. However, it also has other benefits. It creates circulation, thus helps to maintain an even water temperature throughout the aquarium. In so doing it takes unwanted gases, such as carbon dioxide and ammonia, to the water surface where they dissipate into the atmosphere. The equipment used to aerate the tank can also have the effect of creating a pleasing appearance as the bubbles of air rise to the surface.

◆ There is no better gift than an aquarium. It teaches children love of nature, respect for living things and responsibility. The life of the fish depends on their care.

Susan is too young to care for her own tank, but Mother Vallerie is showing her the cichlids as they spawn. Susan studied the eggs, fry and eventually the adults and learned a lot about nature. ◆

◆ Hagen has a do-it-yourself undergravel filter. The bottom blocks fit together to fit any aquarium you might have.

◆ Pre-formed undergravel filters are available from Hagen for bowls (round) as well as rectangular tanks. Before you buy the filter, you must know the dimensions of the tank bottom.

Filtration

Of itself aeration will ensure that the fish have ample oxygen (as long as you do not go overboard in stocking the aquarium), but it will do little to maintain the water quality. It will help remove unwanted gases, but that still leaves a great number of pollutants in the water. To overcome this situation you must install some sort of filter system that will help keep the water clean and healthy.

The basis of a filter system is that the water is passed through a container which houses differing filter media. The filtering media trap large and small solid pollutants. The cleansed water is then returned to the tank, sometimes via a spray bar, and in so doing it creates surface agitation, thus oxygenating the water. A filter system can be of a very basic type, or it can be highly complex, depending on the extent of work it is expected to do and how clear and healthy you wish the water to be.

You can purchase a simple air lift system that works on a siphon basis, but you are much better off with a mechanical arrangement that pumps the water. This will be far more efficient and is not very costly at the bottom end of the market range. With some filters, a pump draws the water from the tank and pushes it through the filter media. There are in-tank filter systems, but as these take up valuable space and are not as easy to service, most aquarists will use an external system. One of the basic forms is attached to the side or back of the tank. There also are canister filters that can be conveniently hidden in a cupboard, or similar enclosure, near the tank. You can also purchase an undergravel biological filter.

Water Chemistry

It is not at all essential that you must understand the many complex chemical reactions that are continually taking place in an aquarium. However, for the well being of the fish there are a few basic aspects that you need to appreciate, at least to the degree that you know how to test for them. Thereafter, you may add to your knowledge according to your interests in the subject of water chemistry.

Faucet (Tap) Water

As you are aware, all faucet water is variously treated in order that it is safe for you to drink. Some of the additives may not harm you but may seriously affect the health of creatures as small as fish. Chlorine is one such additive. To remove this is not a problem and can be done in one of two ways. Either you can pour the water intended for your tank into a bucket and vigorously stir this periodically over a few hours. The chlorine will then dissipate into the air. Alternatively, you can add tablets from your aquatic dealer to the water, after which it can then immediately be used.

It is also wise to run the faucet for a few seconds so that any residual metals, especially copper, that may be in it from the pipes or storage tank are removed. This comment is especially applicable when you have returned from a vacation and the water has thus been standing in the pipes for some time.

The pH of Water

Without going into the chemistry of ions, the pH of water is an indication of its acidic or alkaline state. A scale of 0-14 is used to measure the pH. Readings under 7 are acidic, those over this being alkaline. The number 7 is

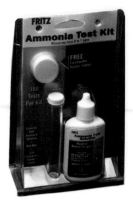

◆ Fritz manufactures a complete line of water test kits. This kit measures the amount of poisonous ammonia in the aquarium water.

◆ There are electronic pH meters available. See them at your local pet shop. Photo courtesy of American Marine, Inc.

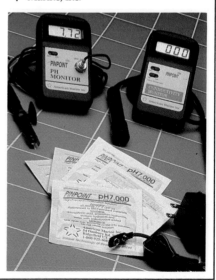

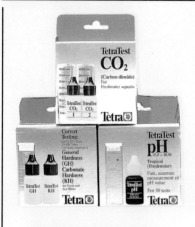

regarded as being neutral. The water in your faucet will normally range from pH 7.0-7.5, so is slightly alkaline. This is just about right for the average community tank of livebearers. Any marble or calcium based material in the water will tend to increase the alkaline state, but CO_2 produced during fish and plant metabolism will tend to neutralize this. They will increase the acidic state of the water, as will any rotting vegetable matter.

You can easily test for the water pH using one of many kits available from your pet store.

Water Hardness

The hardness of water is determined by the amount of salts, such as calcium, magnesium, etc., that are in it. A simple indication of hardness is whether or not your soap lathers easily, which indicates softness, or whether kettles tend to fur, which indicates hardness. There is a loose relationship between water hardness and pH, so that acidic water is normally soft, and alkaline is hard. Livebearers prefer water that is slightly alkaline, which means the water will be moderately hard.

Top, Tetra/Second Nature supplies test kits for pH, carbon dioxide and hardness. *Middle,* It is possible to build aquariums into your walls, but you must have access to them through the back. *Left,* Who says fish aren't pets! Cichlids are easy to train to eat from your hands.

Lighting & Heating

The use of artificial lighting over your aquarium is almost obligatory for a number of reasons. Unlike natural daylight it allows you to easily control the intensity of light to meet your particular tank's needs. It also means you are able to see your fish to the best advantage.

Fluorescent Lighting

There are many forms of lighting you could use, such as tungsten and the various spotlights, but at least initially your choice should be fluorescent lights. These come in many forms, each producing light that is equivalent to certain bands of the light spectrum.

Light Duration & Intensity

The duration of the lighting is a matter of some importance because it will obviously control both the plant and algal growths. This said, duration alone is not the only factor that must be considered. Some plants prefer strong lighting, some like it diffused, and others are happy in dim conditions. The depth of the tank will affect the amount of light that can reach the lower levels, so the intensity of the light is also a factor.

Fluorescent lights have a life of 7500 hours, compared to 750 for a tungsten bulb. They produce little heat, a decided advantage for an aquarium.

Over a period of time the light output of a fluorescent tube will decrease somewhat. Therefore, it is best to replace tubes periodically, even though they are still functioning. It is also very important that the glass cover is kept very clean, or the benefits of your lights will be

◆ A built-in aquarium serves as a living picture and table.

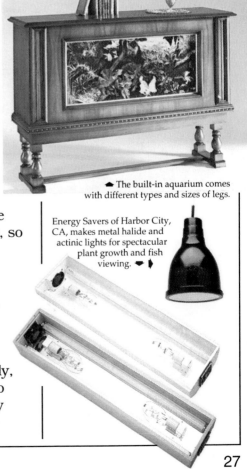

◆ The built-in aquarium comes with different types and sizes of legs.

Energy Savers of Harbor City, CA, makes metal halide and actinic lights for spectacular plant growth and fish viewing. ◆ ▮

Stick-On Thermometers by Hagen attach to the outside glass of the aquarium. ◗

This outside heater attaches to the rim of the aquarium. The top must be kept dry and out of the water.

Hagen makes a Thermal Pre-Set Aquarium Heater line of submersible heaters. ➧

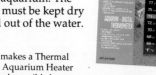

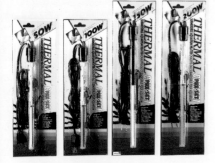

A normal heater attaches to the rim of the tank. ◗

dramatically reduced in terms of plant growth.

Heating

Modern heaters usually come combined with a thermostat and are preset to operate in the range of temperatures most suited to tropical fish. They will have an adjustment switch so you can select your preferred setting. Select a model that features a pilot light to indicate that it is working. Heaters may be of the fully or partially submersible types, the former being the most popular. There are in fact many models to choose from, including those which have the thermostat external to the tank and controlled by micro-chip sensors that are fitted to the glass panels. You should select the heater wattage to broadly match the capacity of your tank.

In a small tank a single heater is usually adequate, but in the larger tank it is often wise to feature two heaters. If one fails the other will prevent a total heat loss. As it happens, the larger the volume of water, the longer the time it will retain its heat.

The power of the heater can be based on the rate of 5 watts per gallon for tanks smaller than 50 US gals, which would cover most likely beginners' needs. A 25 gallon tank would thus need a heater wattage of 125. However, heaters do not come in small increments, so it is a case of using the one that most nearly equates that desired—or using two of a lower wattage to attain the same effect. When siting the heater it is best placed at that point which will give the best even circulation of heat. If two are used, place these at opposite ends of the tank. Always be sure the glass casing is never touching the substrate, otherwise this could create local heating of the glass, thus a breakage. It is wise to include at least one thermometer in or on the aquarium so that you can regularly check that the temperature is as it should be.

Planting the Aquarium

In order to create the completed aquarium look you will want to feature a range of plants. These are important furnishings in any community tank that contains small fish. In the wild habitat such fish will never wander far from stands of plants, because these provide security from predators as well as being places that the fish can browse in—an important part of piscine sociology.

As with other tank furnishings, you can feature both real and artificial plants, though of course the latter do not provide any biological function in respect of water quality (but they do provide a site for beneficial nitrobacteria to colonize). However, the use of artificial plants has gained more respectability over the years because their quality has greatly improved. They enable you to feature certain exotic plants that might otherwise be very difficult to establish in the aquarium.

◄ Tetra supplies fertilizers and a complete line of products that make growing plants easier and more successful.

Fish Foods

Given the tremendous amounts of cash invested in the nutritional requirements of aquarium fish, it is not surprising that commercial foods are generally of a very high standard. Further, there is now an almost bewildering range of products from which you can choose. These may be in various forms, such as flakes, tablets, pellets, pastes, powder, cubes, freeze dried, frozen, liquid, and of course live foods.

The most important rule of all where the feeding of fish is concerned is that they must never be overfed. Obesity is a general problem in all domestic pets. Uneaten food will sink to the bottom where it will decay and

Hikari of Japan makes a complete line of PELLETIZED fish foods. These foods are much different than flake foods and once your fishes become accustomed to them, they will thrive at a much lower cost to you.
➤

▶ Be sure that your undergravel filter fits snugly on the bottom of your tank.

Cover the undergravel filter with sand or gravel. Colored gravels are available through most pet shops. ➤

The Hagen Aquarium Starter Kit might well be the cheapest way to start...and to be sure you have everything you need. ➤

increase the pollution of the water.

Setting-Up

1. If the space behind the tank is restricted, and if a panorama is to be used, this should be placed into position on the rear panel.

2. The tank is now placed into position. The surface for it should be very flat. It is recommended that you place some polystyrene under the tank in order to compensate for any slightly uneven areas of the surface. The pressure of water in only a modest tank is considerable, so there must be no weak spots where the glass is not in contact with the supporting surface.

3. If an undergravel filter is to be fitted, this must be the next item placed into the tank. Be sure it is a very snug fit. If needed, you can apply aquarium seal to any gaps around the edges. The airlift tube must also fit securely. If a powerhead is to be used there may be a need to trim some of the uplift tube in order that the powerhead fits under the glass cover of the aquarium.

4. You may decide to place a plastic mesh grid over the filter: if so, this should be next.

5. Place a layer of gravel over the entire aquarium floor to a depth of about 2.5cm (1in).

6. Now you can add any terracing or plastic gravel retainers at strategic points. The larger rocks and furnishings can also be bedded into the substrate at this time.

7. If you intend to place living plants into the substrate, a layer of peat or other fertilizer can be added.

8. The remaining substrate gravel can now be placed into the tank. It should be built up to a depth of at least 7.5cm (3in) at the rear.

9. The heater can now be placed into the tank and secured with suction cups to the rear glass panel. Thermometers can also be placed into position.

10. The filter intake can be secured a bit above the gravel so that it draws the dirtiest water up. Airstones can be sited toward the back of the tank. Be sure no equipment is plugged into a power socket at this stage.

11. Water can now be poured into the tank so that it fills about 25% of the volume. In order that the gravel is not disturbed it is best to pour it from a jug onto a saucer or a thick piece of cardboard that is placed on the substrate.

12. You can now add the plants and any other smaller decorations. Be sure the plants are well secured in the substrate. Weights in the form of ceramic beads can be used to assist in this aspect. Press any plant feeding tablets into the substrate near the plant roots.

13. The external filter, whether it is of the box type or the canister type, should now be sited in its final position.

14. The remainder of the tank can now be filled with water that has been heated to a little above room temperature. This can be done by adding water boiled in a kettle to the water you have ready in a bucket. Add the water conditioning tablets. Fill the tank to just below the level of the glass cover.

15. The glass cover can now be installed and the canopy containing the lights fitted to the tank. Handle this with great care as it is rather heavy.

16. With everything in place you can now plug in the equipment and, all being well, everything will function. The first thing you will be watching for is that the heater takes the water to the desired temperature. It is useful if you make a note of the time this takes. There is little point in testing for the pH and other things until the water is at the required temperature. You can purchase bacteria cultures from your dealer, or you can add scraps of fish or meat to the water; these will help to start the denitrifying process.

← Don't fill the tank to the top; you almost always have to put your hands into the tank to adjust something. If the tank were filled, it would overflow when you put your hand in.

← Suction cups allow you to put these thermometers wherever you want to.

← The fishes should be put into the new tank carefully, but be sure your tank is ready for them and that the bacterial culture is thriving.

Leopard fantail guppy.

Gold throwback guppy.

Two strains of double swordtail guppies.

Gold snakeskin veiltail guppy.

Red flame veiltail guppy.

During the first couple of weeks you will find, if you conduct water quality tests, that the nitrite levels will rise and then fall, this being quite normal. You may also find some algal blooms at this stage, because algae can become established more quickly than can the plants. It is because the conditions need to stabilize that it is recommended to not include fish for at least two weeks, though I know some people do place one or two hardy fish in almost from the word go. At the end of the first week you can siphon about a third of the tank water away and replace it. Thereafter, you can replace about 20% of the water every second week. This ensures that if any unwanted compounds in solution do get through the filter system they are being continually held in check by the dilution effect of the water changes.

Stocking the Tank

When you are satisfied that the water conditions are becoming stable you can add one or two hardy fish, such as guppies. These will be supplied in a bag of water which can be floated in your aquarium for about thirty minutes. This allows the water temperature in the bag to equate to that of the tank water; then balance the water chemistry by slowly mixing water from the tank with the bag water. You can then slowly open the neck of the bag and let the fish swim gently out. Subsequent fish should only be added one or two at a time over the following couple of months. This allows the stocking rate to build in relation to the filter and biological systems' ability to cope with the fecal matter and other products of metabolism.

Now you need a book and a *Tropical Fish Hobbyist Magazine* to help you select the fishes you want to keep in your aquarium. Your local pet shop has these books and magazines.